Title: The Breakthrough Journey:

"A 12-Week Roadmap to Breaking Down Barriers & Cracking the Code to Success"

<u>Devotional</u>

By D. A. Daniel

Introduction: A Journey of Breakthroughs and Transformation

Dear Reader:

Welcome to the Devotional "The Breakthrough Journey: A 12-Week Roadmap to Breaking Down Barriers and Cracking the Code to Success." I am thrilled that you have chosen to embark on this adventure of self-discovery, growth, and breakthroughs. In the next twelve weeks, this transformative journey is designed to empower you as we will dive deep into the principles and truths that will enable you to experience breakthroughs in every area of your life, aligning your path with God's purpose and unlocking the extraordinary possibilities He has for you in order to crack the code to the success that was meant for you!

Throughout this devotional, you will experience a transformational journey with God as your guide and companion. Together, we will navigate through challenges, unlock hidden potentials, and uncover the abundant blessings that await you.

Each week, you will embark on a new leg of the journey, filled with captivating roadmaps, holy adventures, and practical self-help activities. Along the way, you will find spaces to document your reflections, insights, and progress. Remember, this is not just a reading experience, but an opportunity to engage with God and actively participate in your own breakthrough

Overview: In this devotional, we will embark on an adventure of self-discovery, spiritual growth, and personal transformation. We will also delve into a specific aspect of the Breakthrough Equation, exploring its principles, applying them to our lives, and witnessing the power of God's transformational work. Along the way, we will encounter Scripture, adventure maps (guided steps in the journey toward your goals), self-help activities, reflection points, learning nuggets of wisdom and bonus points.

Purpose: The purpose of this e-devotional is to provide you with practical tools and spiritual insights to break through barriers, overcome obstacles, and experience God's breakthroughs in your life. I want to help you unlock the potential within you, discover your purpose, and step into a life of abundance and fulfillment. Whether you are facing challenges in your career, relationships, personal growth, or spiritual journey. This devotional will equip and empower you to navigate through them with faith, resilience, and divine wisdom.

Inside this Devotional:

- ***12 weeks of transformative teachings:*** Each week will focus on a specific theme, diving deep into the principles of the Breakthrough Equation and offering practical steps for application.

- ***Scriptures for meditation:*** Each week will begin with a scripture passage that sets the foundation for our exploration and serves as a guiding light on our journey.

- ***Self-help activities:*** Engage in practical exercises and self-reflection activities that will help you implement the principles discussed and apply them to your own life.

- ***Reflection points:*** At the end of each chapter, you will find reflection points that encourage introspection, prayer, and journaling. These moments of contemplation will deepen your understanding, facilitate personal growth, and foster a closer relationship with God.

- ***Learning Nuggets of Wisdom:*** Each week will conclude with a nugget of wisdom from the author, offering further insights and encouragement to carry with you on your journey.

To make the most of this devotional, here's a checklist of tips for effective use:

1. *Set aside dedicated time:* Carve out a specific time each day or week to engage with the devotional content and activities.

2. *Create a sacred space:* Designate a quiet and peaceful space where you can fully immerse yourself in reflection, prayer, and study.

3. *Bring your journal:* Keep a journal handy to record your thoughts, prayers, and insights throughout the journey. Document your progress and revelations as you navigate each week.

4. *Embrace self-reflection:* Take the time to honestly assess your current circumstances, challenges, and desires for breakthrough. Be open to personal growth and transformation.

5. *Engage in prayer and meditation:* Seek God's presence as you delve into each chapter. Pray for guidance, wisdom, and a receptive heart to receive His breakthroughs in your life.

6. *Participate in self-help activities:* Actively engage in the practical exercises and self-reflection activities provided. Apply the principles discussed to your own life and observe the positive changes that unfold.

7. *Seek accountability:* Consider sharing your journey with a trusted friend or mentor who can provide support, encouragement, and accountability throughout the devotional.

8. *Stay committed:* Commit to completing the 12-week journey, even when faced with challenges or distractions. Remember that breakthroughs require persistence, faith, and perseverance.

Throughout this devotional, we invite you to approach each week with an open heart and a willingness to be transformed. Prepare to embrace new perspectives, step out in faith, cultivate resilience, express gratitude, and embark on a personal journey of growth and breakthroughs.

As the author of this devotional, I want to assure you of my love, prayers, and heartfelt encouragement. May this journey be a source of inspiration, empowerment, and spiritual growth. Trust that God is with you every step of the way, guiding, strengthening, and equipping you for the breakthroughs that lie ahead.

May this devotional serve as a roadmap, guiding you towards a life of purpose, joy, and extraordinary breakthroughs. As you walk this path, know that you are not alone. God is with you every step of the way, ready to pour out His blessings and lead you to the abundant life He has prepared for you.

Get ready to crack the code to success and experience the breakthroughs you've been longing for. Let's begin this life-changing adventure together!

With love and blessings,

D. A. Daniel

Table of Contents

Revision Exercise

Before we move forward, let's take a quick and concerted look at what was discussed in the book, "The Breakthrough Equation: Cracking the Code to Success".

Let's start with and/or remind ourselves of what the Breakthrough Code is according to the Book:

The Breakthrough Code: Cracking the Code to Success is a comprehensive guidebook that presents a proven system and set of principles for achieving remarkable breakthroughs in life. It encompasses a collection of strategies, mindset shifts, and actionable steps that empower individuals to unlock their full potential, overcome obstacles, and create lasting success.

By cracking the code, individuals gain access to the secrets of personal growth, spiritual alignment, goal attainment, and transformative change. It is a transformative resource that equips individuals with the tools and knowledge to navigate challenges, tap into their innate strengths, and experience breakthroughs in every area of life. Let us briefly look at what was examined in the various chapters of the book.

Chapter 1: The Foundation of Faith

- Unleashing the Power of Belief: Exploring the profound impact that belief has on our lives and how it shapes our reality.
- Cultivating a Strong Spiritual Foundation: Nurturing a deep connection with God through prayer, meditation, and spiritual practices.

- Harnessing Faith as the Catalyst for Breakthroughs: Understanding how faith can propel us forward, fuel our dreams, and overcome obstacles on the path to success.

Chapter 2: The Equation of Prayer

- The Transformative Power of Prayer: Discovering the profound effects of prayer on our mindset, emotions, and actions.
- Building a Deep Connection with God: Establishing a consistent and meaningful prayer practice to strengthen our relationship with God.
- Aligning Your Desires with the Will of God: Learning to surrender and seek guidance, aligning our goals and aspirations with God's purpose for our lives.

Chapter 3: The Variable of Persistence

- Embracing Perseverance in the Face of Challenges: Examining the role of persistence in overcoming obstacles and staying committed to our goals.
- Overcoming Obstacles through Determination: Strategies for staying resilient, bouncing back from setbacks, and maintaining focus on our vision.
- Nurturing Resilience on the Journey to Success: Cultivating resilience through self-care, positive mindset, and learning from failures to propel us forward.

Chapter 4: The Element of Purpose

- Discovering Your Life's Purpose and Calling: Reflecting on our passions, talents, and values to uncover our unique purpose in life.

- Aligning Your Goals with Divine Purpose: Understanding how aligning our goals with a higher purpose can bring clarity, motivation, and fulfillment.
- Living a Purpose-Driven Life for Breakthroughs: Exploring the transformative power of living in alignment with our purpose and making a meaningful impact on the world.

Chapter 5: The Formula of Gratitude

- Cultivating an Attitude of Gratitude: Embracing gratitude as a daily practice to shift our perspective, attract abundance, and enhance well-being.
- The Power of Appreciation and Thankfulness: Understanding how expressing gratitude for what we have unlocks doors to greater blessings and opportunities.
- Opening Doors of Abundance through Gratefulness: Exploring practical ways to infuse gratitude into our lives and harness its transformative power for breakthroughs.

Chapter 6: The Adventure of Laughter

- Unlocking the Power of Holy Humor: LOL - Love Our Laughter! Embrace the transformative power of laughter as a gift from God. Allow humor to bring lightness and joy to your life, fostering deeper connections with others and nurturing a positive outlook.
- Finding Joy Amidst Trials: Don't Let Life's Potholes Steal Your Smile! Choose to find joy even in the midst of challenging circumstances. Shift your perspective and focus on gratitude, cultivating a resilient spirit that can withstand life's ups and downs.

- The Power of a Cheerful Heart: Smiling Your Way to Success- Harness the power of a cheerful heart as you go through your intentional process towards success and abundance. Cultivate a positive attitude, radiating joy and optimism in your interactions with others, and watch as it opens doors to new opportunities and blessings.

Chapter 7: The Ingredient of Service

- The Joy and Fulfillment of Serving Others: Recognizing the profound impact of selfless acts of service on our well-being and overall sense of fulfillment.
- Making a Difference and Impacting Lives: Exploring different ways to contribute to the well-being of others, communities, and the world.
- Unleashing Breakthroughs through Acts of Service: Understanding how serving others not only benefits them but also opens doors for personal growth, success, and breakthroughs.

Chapter 8: The Sum of Self-Reflection

- Embracing Self-Awareness and Personal Growth: The importance of self-reflection in gaining clarity, understanding our strengths and weaknesses, and evolving as individuals.
- Evaluating Progress and Adjusting Course: Developing the habit of regularly assessing our goals, measuring progress, and making necessary adjustments to stay on track.

- Celebrating Achievements and Setting New Goals: Reflecting on our accomplishments, expressing gratitude, and setting new goals to continuously strive for breakthroughs and success.

Conclusion: Living the Breakthrough Equation

- Integrating the Elements for Lasting Success: Understanding how the different components of faith, prayer, persistence, purpose, gratitude, service, and self-reflection work together synergistically for lasting success and fulfillment.
- Embracing a Life of Abundance and Fulfillment: Embodying the principles discussed in the book to create a life of abundance, purpose, and meaning.
- Inspiring Others to Unlock Their Breakthroughs: Using our own journey and experiences to inspire and uplift others, empowering them to discover and unlock their own breakthroughs.

In essence, The Breakthrough Code assists with unraveling the blueprint to phenomenal success and serves as an empowering compass, leading individuals on an exhilarating voyage towards unlocking their limitless potential and achieving extraordinary triumphs. This transformative guidebook intertwines an array of groundbreaking strategies, paradigm shifts, and tangible action steps, enabling individuals to conquer obstacles, tap into their inner reservoirs of strength, and engineer profound breakthroughs in every facet of their lives.

By embracing the profound principles of The Breakthrough Code, readers are impeccably equipped with an arsenal of tools and wisdom to unleash their truest capabilities, embrace a purpose-driven existence, and ignite a ripple effect of inspiration that emboldens others to embark on their own remarkable odyssey to greatness!

Week 1: Embracing Faith - Setting the Foundation

Scripture: "Trust in the LORD with all your heart, and do not lean on your own understanding. In all your ways acknowledge him, and he will make straight your paths." - Proverbs 3:5-6

Embracing Faith - Setting the Foundation is a transformative journey that calls us to anchor our lives on the solid rock of Jesus Christ and faith in Him. As we delve into the spiritual truths of the Holy Scriptures, we discover that faith is not merely a passive belief, but an active power that propels us towards miraculous breakthroughs. It is a powerful conviction that fuels our actions and aligns our hearts with God's purpose. By nurturing a strong foundation of faith, we cultivate a profound trust in God's and His promises given through the Holy Bible which is God's word, empowering us to overcome obstacles, pursue our dreams with unwavering determination, and experience the abundant life that He has destined for us. As we embark on this chapter, may we be inspired to step out in faith, surrendering our doubts and fears, and embracing the limitless possibilities that await us when we place our trust in the hands of our faithful and loving Creator.

Adventure Map:

1. *The Road to Trust: Surrendering to God's Plan*

    - Reflect on areas of your life where you struggle to trust God fully. Write them down and commit to surrendering them to Him.

- Engage in prayer, surrendering your plans and desires to God. Trust Him to guide your path.

2. *Faith Mountains: Overcoming Doubts and Fears*

   - Identify any doubts or fears that hinder your faith. Write them down and pray for God's strength to overcome them.
   - Meditate on God's faithfulness by recalling past moments when He has proven Himself trustworthy.

3. *Direction Signs: Seeking God's Guidance*

   - Set aside time each day for seeking God's guidance through prayer and meditation.
   - Listen attentively to God's voice through His Word, seeking His direction in decision-making and life choices.

4. *Believing Beyond Sight: Walking in Faith*

   - Memorize and meditate on Proverbs 3:5-6, reminding yourself to trust in God's guidance.
   - Step out in faith, taking courageous actions aligned with God's purpose for your life.

5. *Destination Celebration: Grateful for God's Faithfulness*

   - Reflect on past breakthroughs and blessings, expressing gratitude to God for His faithfulness.

- Share your testimony of God's faithfulness with others, encouraging them in their faith journey.

Learning Nugget of Wisdom: "Faith is the compass that aligns your heart with God's purpose, guiding you on the path to breakthroughs. Embrace faith, and watch how God turns impossibilities into possibilities."

Bonus: Reflect on a time when God's faithfulness was evident in your life. Write a thanksgiving prayer expressing gratitude for His faithfulness.

Week 2: The Power of Prayer Part 1- Connecting with God, The Navigator

Scripture: "Ask, and it will be given to you; seek, and you will find; knock, and it will be opened to you." - Matthew 7:7

The Power of Prayer - Connecting with God as our divine navigator is a transformative exploration of the profound impact of prayer in our lives. Through prayer, we establish a direct line of communication with God, tapping into the infinite wisdom and guidance of our Heavenly Navigator. It is a sacred conversation where we pour out our hearts, share our hopes and dreams, seek divine intervention, and surrender our burdens.

As we delve into the spiritual truths of the Holy Scriptures, we uncover the transformative power of prayer to align our desires with the will of God, to experience peace amidst chaos, and to witness miracles unfold in our lives. By cultivating a deep and intimate connection through prayer, we open ourselves up to receive divine guidance, strength, and comfort, empowering us to navigate the storms of life with unwavering faith and confidence.

As we embark on this chapter, may our hearts be ignited with a fervent desire to seek the face of our Divine Navigator, knowing that in His presence, we find solace, direction, and the power to overcome any obstacle that comes our way.

Adventure Map:

1. *The Prayer Path: Building a Foundation of Communication*

   - Dedicate specific time each day for prayer and meditation. Journal your prayers and any insights received.
   - Reflect on the importance of communication with God and how it deepens your relationship with Him.

2. *Heavenly Conversations: Deepening Your Prayer Life*

   - Explore different prayer methods such as intercession, thanksgiving, and supplication.
   - Experiment with prayer tools like prayer journals, prayer lists, or prayer prompts to enhance your prayer life.

3. *Prayer Warriors: Unleashing the Power of Intercession*

   - Identify individuals or causes in need of prayer. Commit to interceding for them regularly.
   - Engage in spiritual warfare through prayer, binding negative influences and declaring God's victory.

4. *Divine GPS: Seeking God's Guidance through Prayer*

   - Learn to discern God's voice through prayer and meditation on His Word.
   - Practice listening in prayer, allowing God to guide your steps and reveal His plans for your life.

5. *Breakthrough Declarations: Speaking God's Promises*

- Discover and declare God's promises over your life, aligning your words with His truth.
- Develop a habit of speaking life-affirming declarations that reinforce your faith and break through barriers.

Self-Help Activities:

- Set aside dedicated time each day for prayer and meditation. Journal your prayers and any insights received.
- Create a prayer list of personal intentions and the needs of others. Commit to interceding for them regularly.
- Memorize Matthew 7:7 and recite it throughout the day, reminding yourself of the power of prayer.

Learning Nugget of Wisdom: "Prayer is the bridge that connects your heart to the heart of God. Embrace prayer as a powerful tool for breakthroughs and watch how God moves in your life."

Bonus: Take a moment to write down a testimony of a specific prayer that God has answered in your life. Use it as a reminder of His faithfulness and a source of encouragement during challenging times.

Week 3: The Adventure of Laughter - Joyful Steps to Breakthroughs

Scripture: "A joyful heart is good medicine, but a crushed spirit dries up the bones." - Proverbs 17:22

The Adventure of Laughter - Joyful Steps to Breakthroughs is an exhilarating exploration of the transformative power of laughter in our lives. Through the lens of joy and humor, we embark on a journey that brings lightness and positivity into every aspect of our being. As we embrace the power of holy humor, we unlock the gates to joy, allowing laughter to permeate our souls and radiate through our lives. In the midst of life's trials and challenges, we refuse to let the potholes steal our smiles, finding resilience and strength in the joy that comes from within. With a cheerful heart, we navigate the path to success, realizing that a genuine smile can open doors, uplift others, and bring us closer to our breakthroughs. Let us embark on this adventure of laughter, ready to embrace the joy, spread the laughter, and unlock the transformative power that awaits us on this delightful journey.

Adventure Map:

1. *The Laughter Highway: Rediscovering the Gift of Laughter*

   - Reflect on the joy and laughter that God has placed in your life. Write down moments of laughter and gratitude.
   - Explore activities that bring you joy, such as watching a comedy show or spending time with loved ones.

2. *Comedy Stops: Finding Joy Amidst Trials*

- Identify challenging situations you're currently facing. Look for opportunities to find humor and joy within them.
- Share lighthearted moments with others, spreading laughter and joy.

3. *Humor Detour: Embracing Light-heartedness*

- Cultivate a light-hearted perspective by focusing on the positive, finding humor in everyday situations.
- Share funny stories or jokes with friends and family, creating an atmosphere of joy and laughter.

4. *Laughter Workouts: Exercising Your Joy Muscles*

- Engage in activities that naturally make you laugh, such as watching funny videos or reading humorous books.
- Practice laughter or deep belly laughs to release stress and tension, fostering a joyful mindset.

5. *Celebration Junction: Cultivating a Lifestyle of Joy*

- Celebrate milestones, achievements, and blessings, expressing gratitude to God for His goodness.
- Embrace a mindset of joy, choosing to find delight in the simple pleasures of life.

Self-Help Activities:

- Watch a funny movie or comedy show and allow yourself to laugh freely.

- Keep a "Joy Journal" where you write down moments of laughter and joy each day.

- Share a funny story or joke with a friend or family member to spread laughter.

Learning Nugget of Wisdom: "Laughter is the soundtrack of a joy-filled life. Embrace humor as a source of strength, healing, and breakthroughs in your journey."

Bonus: Create a "Joy Jar" by writing down joyful moments or blessings on small pieces of paper and collecting them in a jar. Whenever you need an extra boost of joy, reach into the jar and read a few notes.

Week 4: Navigating the Wilderness - Overcoming Challenges with God's Strength

Scripture: "I can do all things through him who strengthens me." - Philippians 4:13

Navigating the Wilderness - Overcoming Challenges with God's Strength is a courageous expedition through the rugged terrains of life's trials and tribulations. In this journey, we discover the power of relying on God's strength to conquer obstacles that stand in our way. As we trek through the wilderness, we learn to surrender our weaknesses and embrace the unwavering strength found in our Creator. With each step, we grow in resilience, knowing that we are not alone in our struggles. We find solace in the promises of God's presence and guidance, knowing that He will lead us through the darkest valleys to the mountaintop of victory. Let us boldly venture into the wilderness, equipped with faith, fortified by God's strength, and confident that we will emerge triumphant on the other side.

Adventure Map:

1. *Wilderness Reflections: Embracing Growth in the Midst of Challenges*

   - Reflect on past wilderness experiences and how they shaped your character and faith.

   - Journal your thoughts on how God has provided strength and guidance during challenging times.

2. *Trailblazing Faith: Trusting God's Provision*

   - Identify areas in your life where you struggle to trust God's provision. Surrender those areas to Him in prayer.
   - Seek examples in the Bible of how God provided for His people in the wilderness. Meditate on His faithfulness.

3. *Desert Oasis: Finding Refreshment in God's Word*

   - Dedicate time each day to read and meditate on God's Word, drawing nourishment and encouragement.
   - Memorize Scriptures that remind you of God's faithfulness and strength.

4. *Uphill Battles: Persevering with Endurance*

   - Identify current challenges you're facing. Write down specific ways you can lean on God's strength to overcome them.
   - Seek accountability and support from fellow believers who can pray for you and encourage you on your journey.

5. *Summit Victories: Celebrating Breakthroughs*

   - Reflect on past victories and breakthroughs in your life. Express gratitude to God for His faithfulness.
   - Share your testimonies of overcoming challenges with others, inspiring them to trust in God's strength.

Self-Help Activities:

- Take a nature walk or hike, allowing the beauty of creation to remind you of God's provision and strength.
- Create a visual representation of your current challenge and how you envision overcoming it. Use it as a reminder to rely on God's strength.

Learning Nugget of Wisdom: "In the wilderness, you discover the depth of your reliance on God's strength. Trust in Him, and you will overcome every challenge that comes your way."

Bonus: Take time to reflect on a recent challenge you faced and how God provided the strength needed to overcome it. Write a prayer of thanksgiving for His faithfulness.

Week 5: Unleashing Creativity - Tapping into God's Infinite Imagination

Scripture: "In the beginning, God created..." - Genesis 1:1

Unleashing Creativity - Tapping into God's Infinite Imagination is an exhilarating exploration of the creative depths within us. As we open ourselves to God's divine inspiration, we unlock the door to endless possibilities and innovative breakthroughs. By embracing our unique gifts and talents, we become vessels for God's creativity to flow through us, bringing beauty, innovation, and transformation into the world. In this journey, we learn to silence self-doubt and fear, allowing God's limitless imagination to guide us towards new horizons. Let us dare to dream big, to step outside the boundaries of conventional thinking, and to trust in God's creative power that dwells within us. Together, we will unleash a symphony of innovation and leave an indelible mark on the canvas of life.

Adventure Map:

1. *Divine Imagination: Recognizing the Creator's DNA in You*
   - Reflect on how God's creative nature is reflected in your own life. Journal your unique gifts and talents.
   - Meditate on the truth that you are made in the image of a creative God.

2. *Artistic Inspiration: Exploring Different Forms of Creativity*
   - Engage in activities that spark your creativity, such as painting, writing, singing, or gardening.

- Seek inspiration from God's creation, observing the beauty and intricacy around you.

3. *Breaking Boundaries: Embracing Risk and Innovation*
   - Identify areas in your life where fear of failure hinders your creative expression. Pray for God's courage to step out of your comfort zone.
   - Experiment with new ideas, approaches, or solutions. Embrace the process, knowing that God can turn failures into breakthroughs.

4. *Collaborative Masterpieces: Engaging in Community Creativity*
   - Connect with fellow creatives and collaborate on a project or artistic endeavor.
   - Share your creative journey with others, inspiring and encouraging one another.

5. *Cultivating Beauty: Using Creativity to Reflect God's Glory*
   - Use your creative talents to bring beauty and joy to others. Serve your community through acts of creativity and love.
   - Dedicate time to worship God through creative expression, offering your talents as an act of worship.

Self-Help Activities:
- Set aside dedicated time each week for a creative activity of your choice.

- Keep a creativity journal where you jot down ideas, inspirations, and reflections on your creative journey.

Learning Nugget of Wisdom: "As you unleash your creativity, you tap into the vast ocean of God's imagination. Embrace your creative gifts and watch how God brings forth breakthroughs and beauty."

Bonus: Reflect on a recent creative project or endeavor and document the lessons you learned from the process. Use those insights to guide your future creative pursuits.

Week 6: The Power of Gratitude (Part 1) - Unlocking Abundance and Breakthroughs

Scripture: "Give thanks in all circumstances; for this is the will of God in Christ Jesus for you." - 1 Thessalonians 5:18

The Power of Gratitude - Unlocking Abundance and Breakthroughs reveals the transformative nature of cultivating a grateful heart. As we shift our focus from scarcity to abundance, we open ourselves to the limitless blessings that surround us. By expressing gratitude for both the big and small things in life, we create a positive energy that attracts more blessings and opportunities for growth. This journey teaches us to count our blessings, to cultivate a spirit of appreciation, and to embrace the abundance that is available to us. Through the power of gratitude, we unlock the door to breakthroughs, abundance, and a life filled with joy and fulfillment. Let us embark on this journey of thankfulness and watch as our lives overflow with blessings beyond measure.

Adventure Map:

1. *Gratitude Mindset: Cultivating a Heart of Thanksgiving*

   - Begin each day by expressing gratitude to God for His blessings and provision. Write down three things you're grateful for.
   - Reflect on past challenges and how God's faithfulness has brought breakthroughs. Offer thanks for His guidance and provision.

2. *Gratitude Journaling: Documenting the Gifts of Each Day*

- Keep a gratitude journal where you write down moments of gratitude and blessings throughout the day.
- Review your gratitude journal regularly to remind yourself of God's faithfulness and goodness.

3. *Overflowing Thanksgiving: Expressing Gratitude to Others*

- Choose someone in your life whom you appreciate. Write a heartfelt letter expressing your gratitude and deliver it to them.
- Look for opportunities to express gratitude to others through acts of kindness and encouragement.

4. *Grateful Reflections: Finding Lessons in Every Season*

- Reflect on challenging seasons in your life and seek the lessons and growth that came from them. Write down insights and revelations.
- Thank God for His presence and guidance during those difficult times, knowing that He works all things together for your good.

5. Gratitude in Abundance: Giving Generously

- Practice generosity by giving to others in need. Give financially, donate your time, or offer acts of service to bless others.

- Thank God for the abundance in your life and ask Him to use your resources to bring breakthroughs in the lives of others.

Self-Help Activities:

- Start a gratitude jar where you write down moments of gratitude on small pieces of paper. Add a new note each day.
- Take time each evening to reflect on the day's blessings and offer thanks to God in prayer.

Learning Nugget of Wisdom: "Gratitude opens the door to abundance and breakthroughs. Cultivate a heart of thanksgiving, and watch how God multiplies His blessings in your life."

Bonus: Share a meal or coffee with someone and take turns expressing gratitude for the blessings in your lives. Let this time of fellowship and thanksgiving deepen your relationships.

Week 7: The Power of Prayer Part 2 - Conversations with the Breakthrough Giver (Going to another level in prayer)

Scripture: "Do not be anxious about anything, but in everything by prayer and supplication with thanksgiving let your requests be made known to God." - Philippians 4:6

The Power of Prayer (Going to another level in prayer) - As we delve deeper into connecting with God and strengthening our prayer life, our conversations with the Breakthrough Giver unveils the profound impact of our communication with Him. Through prayer, we enter into a sacred dialogue with the One who holds the keys to breakthroughs and miracles. By cultivating a deep and intimate connection with the Breakthrough Giver, we open ourselves to receive divine guidance, wisdom, and provision. This journey teaches us to surrender our worries, to pour out our hearts in prayer, and to trust in the faithfulness of God. Through the power of prayer and going deeper in and with God in conversations with Him, we experience the miraculous, witness obstacles being removed, and step into the realm of breakthroughs that surpass our wildest dreams. Let us embark on this transformative journey of growing in our prayer life, knowing that our conversations with the Breakthrough Giver have the power to shape our lives and unlock extraordinary possibilities.

Adventure Map:

1. *Prayer as Communion: Deepening Your Relationship with God*

   - Reflect on the significance of prayer as a means of communing with God. Seek to deepen your intimacy with Him through prayer.

- Set aside dedicated time each day for prayer, creating a sacred space for conversation with God.

2. *Prayers of Petition: Bringing Your Needs and Desires to God*
   - Identify specific areas in your life where you need breakthroughs. Write down your prayer requests and surrender them to God.
   - Pray with faith, knowing that God hears your prayers and is actively working on your behalf.

3. *Intercessory Prayer: Standing in the Gap for Others*
   - Choose individuals or situations for which you feel called to pray. Lift them up in intercession, asking God for breakthroughs and blessings.
   - Form or join a prayer group where you can collectively intercede for the needs of others.

4. *Prayers of Gratitude: Thanking God for His Goodness*
   - Offer prayers of gratitude to God for His faithfulness, provision, and answered prayers. Express thanksgiving for His breakthroughs in your life.
   - Develop a habit of gratitude in your prayers, focusing on His goodness even amidst challenges.

5. *Praying God's Promises: Declaring His Word in Faith*

- Identify promises from God's Word that align with your specific needs and breakthroughs. Meditate on these promises and pray them with confidence.
- Declare God's promises over your life, trusting that He will fulfill His Word.

Self-Help Activities:

- Create a prayer journal where you write down your prayers, including requests, answers, and reflections.
- Set aside a dedicated prayer walk or quiet time in nature, allowing the beauty of God's creation to inspire your prayers.

Learning Nugget of Wisdom: "Prayer is the key that unlocks breakthroughs in every area of life. Approach the throne of God with confidence, knowing that He is eager to hear and answer your prayers."

Bonus: Choose a day to engage in a full day of prayer and fasting, seeking breakthroughs in specific areas of your life or for others in need.

Week 8: Embracing God's Timing - Patience and Trust on the Journey

Scripture: "But they who wait for the Lord shall renew their strength; they shall mount up with wings like eagles; they shall run and not be weary; they shall walk and not faint." - Isaiah 40:31

Embracing God's Timing - Patience and Trust on the Journey illuminates the beauty and significance of surrendering to God's timing of our lives. It calls us to let go of our impatience and to trust that God's timing is perfect. In the midst of waiting, we learn valuable lessons of faith, perseverance, and humility. This journey invites us to release our desires and agendas, and to surrender to the higher wisdom and plan of God. As we embrace God's timing with patience and trust, we discover that the waiting period is not wasted, but rather a time of growth, preparation, and transformation. Let us embrace this journey, knowing that in God's appointed time, breakthroughs will unfold, and our lives will be enriched beyond measure.

Adventure Map:

1. *Divine Delays: Understanding the Purpose of Waiting*

   - Reflect on times in your life when you've experienced waiting. Seek to understand the lessons and growth that can come from seasons of waiting.

   - Embrace a posture of trust and surrender, knowing that God's timing is perfect and His plans are for your good.

2. *Resting in His Promises: Anchoring Your Faith in God's Word*

- Identify promises in Scripture that speak to God's faithfulness and His timing. Memorize these promises and meditate on them during times of waiting.

- Write down specific areas of your life where you're currently waiting on breakthroughs. Offer prayers of trust and surrender to God.

3. *Developing Patience: Nurturing a Fruit of the Spirit*

- Reflect on areas of your life where impatience and frustration arise. Pray for the Holy Spirit to cultivate patience within you.

- Practice patience in daily life situations, intentionally choosing to respond with grace and understanding.

4. *Trusting God's Direction: Seeking His Guidance in Decision-Making*

- During times of waiting, seek God's guidance in making decisions. Spend time in prayer and seek wise counsel from trusted mentors or spiritual leaders.

- Trust that God will lead you in the right direction and bring breakthroughs in His perfect timing.

5. *Enjoying the Journey: Finding Joy and Growth in the Waiting Season*

- Embrace the present moment and find joy in the journey, even while waiting for breakthroughs. Look for opportunities to grow and learn during this time.

- Cultivate a heart of gratitude for the lessons and blessings that come with the waiting season.

Self-Help Activities:

- Engage in a creative activity that requires patience, such as painting or gardening. Allow the process to teach you patience and trust.
- Keep a gratitude journal specifically for documenting blessings and growth experienced during waiting seasons.

Learning Nugget of Wisdom: "Waiting is not wasted time but a season of preparation and growth. Trust in God's timing, and you will see breakthroughs beyond what you can imagine."

Bonus: Set aside a day to unplug from technology and spend intentional time in solitude and prayer, seeking God's guidance and finding peace in His presence.

Week 9: Stepping into Courage - Conquering Fear and Taking Bold Actions

Scripture: "Have I not commanded you? Be strong and courageous. Do not be frightened, and do not be dismayed, for the Lord your God is with you wherever you go."

- Joshua 1:9

Stepping into Courage - Conquering Fear and Taking Bold Actions empowers us to overcome our fears and step into a life of boldness and courage. It invites us to confront the limitations that fear imposes on us and to embrace the limitless possibilities that await us on the other side. Through faith and trust in God's strength, we can rise above our insecurities and doubts, and take courageous steps towards our breakthroughs. This journey encourages us to face our fears head-on, knowing that with God by our side, we are capable of achieving greatness. Let us embrace this path of courage, as we step outside our comfort zones, embrace vulnerability, and unleash our full potential.

Adventure Map:

1. *Facing Your Fears: Identifying Barriers to Breakthroughs*

   - Reflect on the fears and insecurities that have held you back from pursuing your dreams. Write them down and surrender them to God.

   - Pray for courage and ask God to reveal His truth about who you are in Him.

2. *Anchored in God's Promises: Finding Strength in His Word*

   - Explore Scripture passages that speak to God's faithfulness, strength, and provision in the face of fear.

- Memorize a verse that inspires courage and repeat it daily as a declaration of faith.

3. *Courageous Action Steps: Setting Goals and Taking Risks*

- Identify specific goals or dreams you've been hesitant to pursue due to fear. Write them down and break them into actionable steps.
- Step out of your comfort zone by taking one bold action toward your goals. Trust God to lead and guide you.

4. *Community of Courage: Surrounding Yourself with Encouragers*

- Seek out a supportive community or accountability partner who will cheer you on and provide encouragement.
- Share your dreams and goals with others who will pray for you and speak life into your journey.

5. *Empowered by God's Spirit: Tapping into Supernatural Courage*

- Pray for the empowerment of the Holy Spirit to infuse you with courage and boldness.
- Trust in the strength of God's Spirit within you to overcome fear and step into breakthroughs.

Self-Help Activities:

- Fear-Exploration Journaling - Take a moment to reflect on the fears holding you back, journaling about their root causes and associated limiting beliefs. Challenge each fear by writing empowering affirmations and commit to taking small, courageous steps towards overcoming them.

- Stepping Out of Your Comfort Zone Identify an area where you've played it safe, set a specific goal that pushes you outside your comfort zone, and create an action plan. Embrace discomfort as a sign of growth, take the first step, and gradually work towards your goal, reminding yourself of the rewards and personal growth awaiting you.

Learning Nugget of Wisdom: "Courage is not the absence of fear but the willingness to take action despite fear. With God as your strength, you can conquer every obstacle and step into breakthroughs."

Bonus: Share your courageous journey with someone close to you. Celebrate the steps you've taken and the growth you've experienced together.

Week 10: The Power of Resilience - Bouncing Back from Setbacks

Scripture: "But he said to me, 'My grace is sufficient for you, for my power is made perfect in weakness.' Therefore I will boast all the more gladly of my weaknesses, so that the power of Christ may rest upon me." - 2 Corinthians 12:9

The Power of Resilience - Bouncing Back from Setbacks teaches us the invaluable skill of bouncing back from life's challenges and setbacks. It reminds us that setbacks are not the end of our journey but rather opportunities for growth and transformation. With resilience, we can navigate through adversity with grace and determination, never losing sight of our goals and dreams. Resilience allows us to adapt, learn from our experiences, and emerge stronger and wiser. As we embrace the power of resilience, we discover our inner strength and capacity to overcome any obstacle that comes our way, ultimately leading us to the breakthroughs we seek.

Adventure Map:

1. *Embracing Resilience: Understanding the Strength Within You*
   - Reflect on past challenges and setbacks you've overcome. Recognize the resilience that resides within you.
   - Affirm your identity as a resilient child of God, capable of bouncing back from any setback.

2. *Learning from Setbacks: Extracting Lessons for Growth*
   - Reflect on recent setbacks or failures and identify the lessons they hold. Write down the insights and wisdom gained from those experiences.

- Pray for discernment to understand how God is using setbacks to shape and mold you.

3. *Resilient Mindset: Cultivating Positive Thinking*

- Choose to focus on positive thoughts and affirmations, even in the face of adversity. Renew your mind with God's truth and promises.
- Practice gratitude and find blessings even in the midst of setbacks.

4. *Overcoming Obstacles: Developing Strategies for Resilience*

- Identify specific obstacles or challenges that have hindered your progress. Create a plan of action to overcome them, seeking God's guidance.
- Seek support from mentors or individuals who have demonstrated resilience in their own lives.

5. *Restoring and Renewing: Self-Care in Resilience*

- Prioritize self-care activities that rejuvenate your mind, body, and spirit. Nurture healthy habits, such as exercise, rest, and spending time in nature.
- Lean on God's strength and find rest in His presence, knowing that He sustains and renews you.

Self-Help Activities:

- Write a letter to yourself, acknowledging your resilience and encouraging yourself to keep moving forward.

- Create a "resilience jar" where you place uplifting quotes, Bible verses, or affirmations. Draw from it whenever you need a boost of resilience.

Learning Nugget of Wisdom: "Resilience is the secret to bouncing back from setbacks. With God's grace and strength, you can overcome any challenge and experience breakthroughs."

Bonus: Choose a day to engage in a personal retreat where you reflect on your journey of resilience and invite God to guide you toward greater breakthroughs.

Week 11: The Power of Gratitude (Part 2) - Continuing to Cultivate a Thankful Heart for Breakthroughs (Continuing in Gratefulness)

Scripture: "Give thanks in all circumstances; for this is the will of God in Christ Jesus for you." - 1 Thessalonians 5:18

The Power of Gratitude Part 2 (Continuing in Gratefulness) - Continuing to cultivate a thankful heart for breakthroughs reminds us of the transformative power of gratitude in our lives. It teaches us to shift our focus from what is lacking to what we have, cultivating a spirit of appreciation and thankfulness. Through gratitude, we unlock a deeper sense of joy, contentment, and abundance. Gratitude opens the doors to breakthroughs by attracting more blessings into our lives and fostering positive relationships. As we cultivate a thankful heart, we discover that even in the midst of challenges, there is always something to be grateful for, and this perspective shift propels us forward on our journey towards breakthroughs.

Adventure Map:

1. *The Attitude of Gratitude: Shifting Your Perspective*

   - Reflect on the power of gratitude in transforming your outlook on life. Recognize the blessings and breakthroughs that gratitude brings.

   - Start each day by expressing gratitude to God for His goodness and faithfulness.

2. *Grateful Reflection: Journaling Your Blessings*

   - Keep a gratitude journal and write down three things you're thankful for each day. Reflect on the goodness of God and His provision.

- Share your gratitude journey with others, spreading a spirit of thankfulness.

3. *Gratitude in Difficult Times: Finding Gems in the Rough*
    - Identify challenging situations or seasons in your life and look for the hidden blessings or lessons within them.
    - Pray for a grateful heart even in the midst of trials, trusting that God is working all things together for your good.

4. *Gratitude in Relationships: Expressing Appreciation to Others*
    - Take time to express gratitude to the people in your life who have made a positive impact. Write letters or notes of appreciation.
    - Cultivate a habit of expressing gratitude and encouragement to others daily.

5. *Gratitude as a Lifestyle: Living with Joyful Contentment*
    - Embrace gratitude as a way of life, continually seeking out reasons to be thankful.
    - Develop a practice of counting your blessings and cultivating contentment in every season.

Self-Help Activities:

- Create a gratitude jar where you write down moments, blessings, or breakthroughs for which you're grateful. Read them when you need a reminder of God's faithfulness.
- Practice random acts of kindness to express gratitude and bring joy to others.

Learning Nugget of Wisdom: "Gratitude is a magnet for breakthroughs. When you cultivate a thankful heart, you open the door for God's blessings to flow abundantly into your life."

Bonus: Dedicate a day to volunteering or serving others in your community, expressing gratitude through acts of kindness.

Week 12: The Journey of Transformation - Becoming the Best Version of Yourself

Scripture: "Do not be conformed to this world, but be transformed by the renewal of your mind, that by testing you may discern what is the will of God, what is good and acceptable and perfect." - Romans 12:2

The Journey of Transformation - Becoming the Best Version of Yourself is a powerful reminder that our journey towards breakthroughs involves a process of personal and spiritual growth and transformation. It encourages us to embrace self-reflection, identify areas for improvement, and commit to continuous self-improvement. Through this journey, we learn to let go of limiting beliefs and behaviors that hold us back and embrace new ways of thinking and being. As we strive to become the best version of ourselves, we align with our true purpose and unlock our full potential. This journey of transformation is not always easy, but it is worth it, as it leads to a closer walk with God, where we get to know Him more, personal fulfillment, inner peace, and the ability to make a positive impact in the world.

Adventure Map:

1. *Embracing Your Identity in Christ: Discovering Your True Worth*

   - Reflect on your identity in Christ and the unique purpose He has for your life. Seek to understand your true worth and value as a child of God.
   - Pray for God's guidance in aligning your life with His plan for your transformation.

2. *Renewing Your Mind: Transforming Thoughts and Beliefs*

    - Identify negative thought patterns or limiting beliefs that hinder your growth. Replace them with God's truth and affirmations of His promises.
    - Meditate on Scripture passages that speak to transformation and renewal of the mind.

3. *Transformative Habits: Cultivating Daily Disciplines*

    - Identify key areas of your life where transformation is needed, such as spiritual growth, relationships, or personal habits. Develop specific action steps for each area.
    - Commit to daily disciplines that align with your desired transformation, such as prayer, Bible study, and intentional acts of kindness.

4. *Accountability and Support: Surrounding Yourself with Transformational Relationships*

    - Seek accountability partners or join a small group where you can share your transformation journey and receive support.
    - Engage in transformative conversations that challenge and inspire you to become the best version of yourself.

5. Celebrating Milestones: Reflecting on Your Transformational Journey

    - Take time to celebrate the milestones and breakthroughs you've experienced on your journey of transformation.

- Journal about the ways in which God has transformed your life and express gratitude for His faithfulness.

Self-Help Activities:

- Create a vision board that represents the best version of yourself and the transformation you desire. Display it in a prominent place as a visual reminder.
- Engage in a personal retreat where you reflect on your transformational journey and seek God's guidance for continued growth.

Learning Nugget of Wisdom: "Transformation is a lifelong journey that begins with a willingness to surrender to God's transformative work within you. Embrace the process, and you will experience breakthroughs beyond your imagination."

Bonus: Write a letter to yourself, reflecting on the transformational journey you've embarked on and expressing excitement for the future breakthroughs yet to come.

Conclusion: The Restorative Path of Peace

Congratulations on completing this 12-week devotional journey, dear reader! Throughout these weeks, we have embarked on an adventure of discovering the Breakthrough Equation and cracking the code to success in our lives. It has been a journey filled with reflection, prayer, self-discovery, and spiritual growth. As we conclude, let's take a moment to reflect on the key insights and transformations we've experienced together.

Week by week, we explored different facets of the Breakthrough Equation and some new tips and strategies as well, diving deep into its principles and applying them to our lives. We learned the importance of aligning our lives with God's timing and embracing His perfect plan for us. We discovered the power of stepping out in faith, trusting in His guidance even when the path seemed uncertain. We cultivated resilience, bouncing back from setbacks with strength and determination. We fostered gratitude, developing a thankful heart that opens the door for breakthroughs. And finally, we embarked on a journey of personal transformation,aiming to become the best version of ourselves through the renewal of our minds.

Each week, we delved into Scriptures that provided a solid foundation for our journey. These divine truths remind us of God's unwavering love, His faithfulness, and His promises for our lives. We've witnessed how His Word has guided us, inspired us, and empowered us to overcome obstacles and experience breakthroughs.

Throughout this devotional, we've also engaged in self-help activities and reflection points that encouraged us to apply the principles to our own lives. We've embarked on personal adventures, keeping a journal of our progress, and embracing transformative habits that align with our desired breakthroughs. These practical steps have empowered us to take action and witness tangible transformations.

As we conclude this journey, my heart is filled with gratitude for the privilege of walking alongside you. I want to remind you that this is just the beginning. The Breakthrough Equation and the wisdom we've gleaned from Scripture, testimonies, and self-help activities are tools that will continue to guide you on your lifelong journey of faith and transformation.

Remember, dear reader, that the Breakthrough Equation is not a one-time formula but a divine invitation to partner with God in every area of your life. It is an ongoing process of surrendering to His plans, aligning your thoughts and actions with His truth, and allowing Him to work in and through you. Trust that He is faithful to fulfill His promises and lead you into the breakthroughs He has prepared for you.

As you conclude this devotional, we want to provide you with some tips to ensure continued growth beyond these 12 weeks.

1. *Stay connected to God: Cultivate a consistent prayer life and maintain an ongoing relationship with God. Seek His guidance, wisdom, and strength in all areas of your life.*

2. *Deepen your study of Scripture: Continue to explore the Word of God. Dive deeper into the passages and verses that resonated with you during this devotional. Let the Bible be your guide and source of inspiration.*

3. *Practice gratitude daily: Develop a habit of gratitude by regularly expressing thankfulness to God for His blessings, breakthroughs, and faithfulness. A grateful heart opens doors to more miracles.*

4. *Seek ongoing personal growth: Never stop pursuing personal growth and self-improvement. Be intentional about reading books, attending seminars, and seeking wisdom from other Christian authors, ministers, and preachers.*

5. *Foster a supportive community: Surround yourself with like-minded individuals who share your desire for spiritual growth. Join a small group, Bible study, or Christian community where you can encourage and be encouraged by others.*

6. *Revisit the devotional: Remember that this devotional can be used again and again. If you feel the need for a refresher or if you encounter new challenges in the future, feel free to embark on this journey once more. Each time, you may discover new insights and experience deeper levels of breakthrough.*

Do know that God has more in store for you as you continue to walk in faith and trust His guidance. Embrace the lessons you have learned, the breakthroughs you have witnessed, and carry them with you as you step into a future filled with purpose, joy, and extraordinary possibilities.

As we part ways, know that I am sending you love, prayers, and heartfelt wishes for continued growth and breakthroughs. May you walk in the fullness of God's blessings, equipped with the wisdom and empowerment gained from this devotional. May you never lose sight of the incredible potential within you to experience breakthroughs in every aspect of your life.

With God as your guide, you are well-equipped to navigate the challenges, embrace the adventures, and experience breakthroughs beyond your imagination. Trust in His timing, lean on His strength, and live with the assurance that He is always with you!

May God's Word, the Breakthrough Equation and the power of cracking the code to success continue to illuminate your path and lead you to the abundant life God has designed for you.

With encouragement, deep gratitude and blessings-

Love Always,

D. A. Daniel

****

End of Devotional